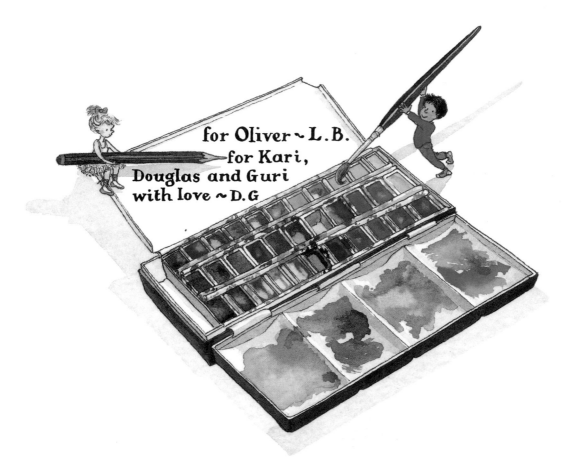

for Oliver ~ L.B.
for Kari,
Douglas and Guri
with love ~ D.G

First U.S. Edition 1993
Text copyright © 1993 by Lisa Bruce
Illustrations copyright © 1993 by Debi Gliori

Bradbury Press
Macmillan Publishing Company
866 Third Avenue
New York, NY 10022

Macmillan Publishing Company is part of the Maxwell Communication Group of Companies.
First published 1993 in Great Britain by Frances Lincoln Ltd., Apollo Works, 5 Charlton Kings Road, London NW5 2SB
England, with the title *Amazing Alphabets*

Printed and bound in Hong Kong
10 9 8 7 6 5 4 3 2 1

LIBRARY OF CONGRESS CATALOGING-IN-PUBLICATION DATA
Bruce, Lisa.
Oliver's alphabets / by Lisa Bruce ; illustrated by Debi Gliori. —
1st U.S. ed.
p.   cm.
Summary: Presents the alphabet using labeled illustrations of
Oliver's friends, toys, instruments, items in his home, and more.
ISBN 0-02-735996-4
1. English language—Alphabet—Juvenile literature.
[1. Alphabet.   2. Vocabulary.]   I. Gliori, Debi, ill.   II. Title.
PE1155.B73   1993
421'.1—dc20   92-39471

Oliver's Alphabets

WRITTEN BY LISA BRUCE
ILLUSTRATED BY DEBI GLIORI

BRADBURY PRESS   New York
Maxwell Macmillan International
New York • Oxford • Singapore • Sydney

Oliver and his friends

Aa	Amy
Bb	Ben
Cc	Charlie
Dd	Darren
Ee	Emily
Ff	Felix
Gg	Gemma
Hh	Hannah
Ii	Ian
Jj	Jamal
Kk	Katy
Ll	Ling
Mm	Maria
Nn	Natasha
Oo	Oscar
Pp	Paul
Qq	Quincy
Rr	Rani
Ss	Sophie
Tt	Tim
Uu	Ursula
Vv	Vijay
Ww	Wendy
Xx	Xusen
Yy	Yolanda
Zz	Zoe

Oliver

Oliver's home

Aa	armchair
Bb	bed
Cc	curtains
Dd	door
Ee	eggs
Ff	fireplace
Gg	grandfather clock
Hh	handlebar
Ii	iron
Jj	jug
Kk	knives
Ll	lamp
Mm	mirror
Nn	nutcracker
Oo	oven
Pp	piano
Qq	quilt
Rr	rug
Ss	sofa
Tt	telephone
Uu	under-the-stairs closet
Vv	vacuum cleaner
Ww	washing machine
Xx	Xerxes the cat
Yy	yogurt
Zz	zipper

Oliver and his friends with their toys

Aa	abacus
Bb	blocks
Cc	cards
Dd	doll
Ee	easel
Ff	fire engine
Gg	garage
Hh	house
Ii	ice skates
Jj	jack-in-the-box
Kk	kite
Ll	lifeboat
Mm	marbles
Nn	necklace
Oo	octopus
Pp	puzzle pieces
Qq	queen's crown
Rr	robot costume
Ss	seesaw
Tt	tea set
Uu	umbrella
Vv	van
Ww	wig
Xx	xylophone
Yy	yo-yo
Zz	zero

Oliver's animals

Aa	ant
Bb	badger
Cc	cow
Dd	duck
Ee	elephant
Ff	fox
Gg	giraffe
Hh	hedgehog
Ii	iguana
Jj	jaguar
Kk	kangaroo
Ll	lion
Mm	mouse
Nn	nanny goat
Oo	owl
Pp	penguin
Qq	quail
Rr	rabbit
Ss	squirrel
Tt	tortoise
Uu	unicorn
Vv	vole
Ww	whale
Xx	x-ray fish
Yy	yak
Zz	zebra

People who work in Oliver's town

Aa   ambulance driver

Bb   builder

Cc   computer operator

Dd   doctor

Ee   electrician

Ff   farmer

Gg   gardener

Hh   hairdresser

Ii   inventor

Jj   jeweler

Kk   kennelmaid

Ll   librarian

Mm   milkman

Nn   nurse

Oo   optician

Pp   policewoman

Qq   quarterback

Rr   road sweeper

Ss   soldier

Tt   teacher

Uu   underwater diver

Vv   veterinarian

Ww   waitress

Xx   x-ray technician

Yy   yachtsman

Zz   zookeeper

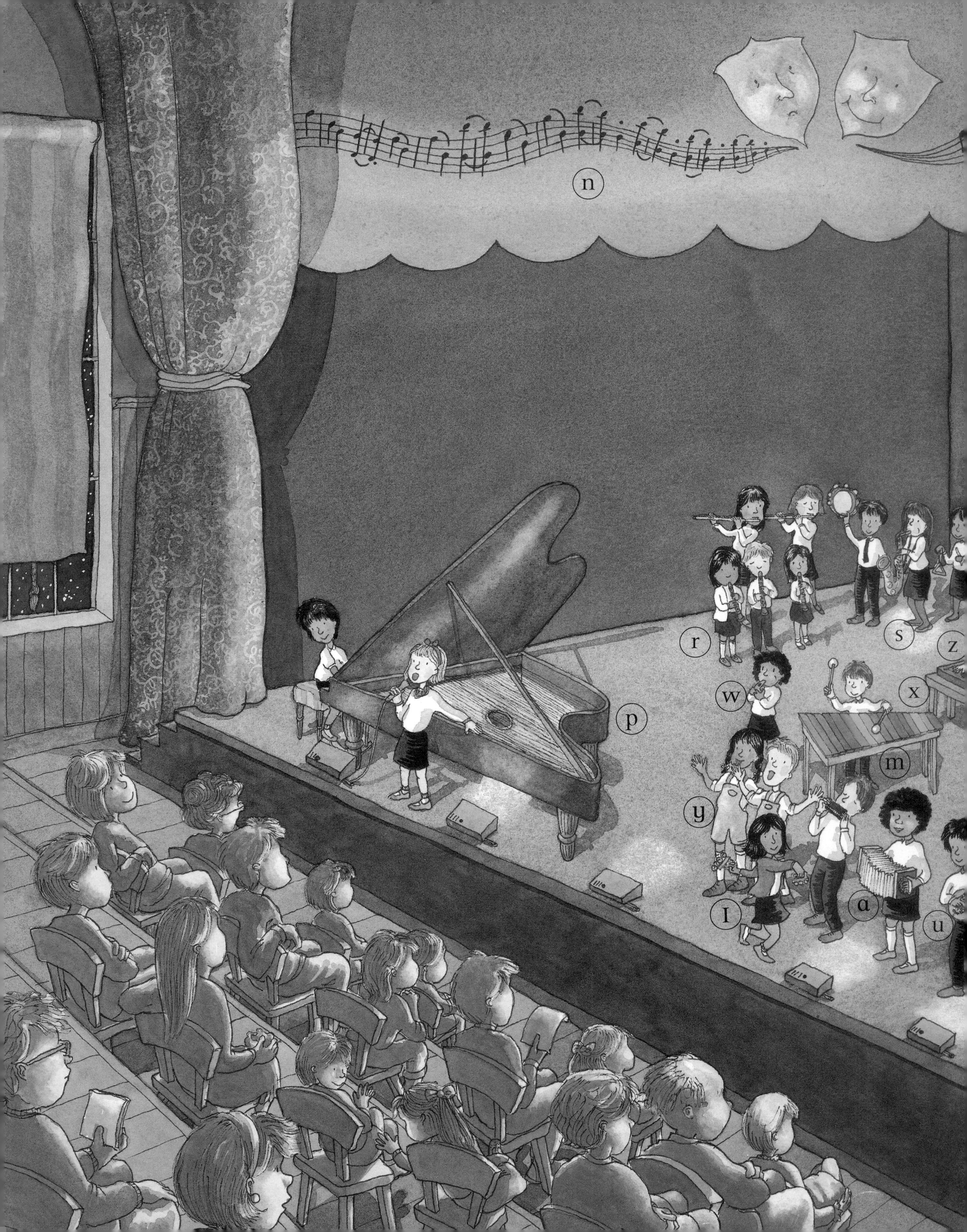
n
p
r
s
z
w
x
m
y
a
l
u

Oliver's orchestra

Aa	accordion
Bb	bass fiddle
Cc	cymbals
Dd	drum
Ee	electronic organ
Ff	French horn
Gg	guitar
Hh	harp
Ii	Indian bells
Jj	jazz band
Kk	keyboard
Ll	lute
Mm	mouth organ
Nn	notes
Oo	oboe
Pp	piano
Qq	quartet
Rr	recorders
Ss	saxophone
Tt	trumpet
Uu	ukelele
Vv	violin
Ww	whistle
Xx	xylophone
Yy	yodelers
Zz	zither

Oliver's holiday

Oliver's birthday party

Aa	airplane
Bb	balloon
Cc	cake
Dd	dog
Ee	Emily
Ff	five
Gg	glove puppet
Hh	hat
Ii	ice cream
Jj	Johnny
Kk	Katy
Ll	lantern
Mm	mask
Nn	napkin
Oo	Oliver
Pp	present
Qq	Quincy
Rr	ribbon
Ss	stairs
Tt	tablecloth
Uu	Ursula
Vv	video camera
Ww	watch
Xx	Xusen
Yy	yellow ball
Zz	Zoe